ODE

TO

LOVE

ODE

TO

LOVE

A JOURNEY OF AWAKENING

SARAH L. DICKEY

ODE TO LOVE

PUBLISHED BY

COOL CREATIVE PRESS
P.O. BOX 238
LISBON, OH 44432
WWW.COOLCREATIVEPRESS.COM

LIBRARY OF CONGRESS CONTROL NUMBER: 2017910195

PUBLISHER'S CATALOGING-IN-PUBLICATION DATA
(PREPARED BY THE DONOHUE GROUP, INC.)

NAMES: DICKEY, SARAH L.
TITLE: ODE TO LOVE : A JOURNEY OF AWAKENING / SARAH L. DICKEY.
DESCRIPTION: LISBON, OH : COOL CREATIVE PRESS, [2018]
IDENTIFIERS: ISBN 978-0-9990720-0-4
SUBJECTS: LCSH: LOVE--POETRY. | SELF-ACTUALIZATION (PSYCHOLOGY)--POETRY.
CLASSIFICATION: LCC PS3604.I35 O34 2018 | DDC 811/.6--DC23

EDITOR: GAIL M. KEARNS, WWW.TOPRESSANDBEYOND.COM
BOOK AND COVER DESIGN: THE BOOK DESIGNERS
BOOK PRODUCTION COORDINATED BY TO PRESS & BEYOND
COOL CREATIVE PRESS LOGO DESIGNED BY STARR STRUCK STUDIO
COVER AND LAYOUT IMAGES USED UNDER LICENSE FROM SHUTTERSTOCK.COM

PRINTED IN THE U.S.A.

TO ALL THE FEARLESS, BADASS, CREATIVE,
IN-PROCESS, VULNERABLE SOULS WHO SAY *YES*.
YES TO THE ENERGY OF LOVE THAT IS GREATER THAN
ANY OF OUR FEARS AND DOUBTS. MAY YOUR LIFE
BECOME AN ODE TO LOVE.

I LOVE YOU BECAUSE YOU ARE A DIVINELY
UNIQUE GIFT FROM THE HEAVENS

GUIDED STRAIGHT TO THE EARTH TO
REMEMBER YOUR ABUNDANT GRACE.

YOUR EMERGENCE HELPS THE WORLD TO
WAKE UP DAY AFTER DAY.

THE SONG OF YOUR LIFE IS ALWAYS ON
MY FAVORITE PLAY LIST.

I LOVE YOU BECAUSE YOU ARE
VULNERABLE AND PURE

A FREE FLOW OF RAW EMOTION
AND ORGANIC EXPRESSION

AN HONEST DECLARATION OF THE
PRESENT MOMENT UNFOLDING

A DELIGHT THAT I EXPERIENCE EACH DAY.

I LOVE YOU INTO THE NIGHT WHEN

YOU SETTLE INTO THE STARS

AND THE LIGHT OF THE MOON ROCKS

YOU IN THE CRADLE OF HER HEART.

I WATCH YOU SLUMBER

AND DREAM A DREAM

AWAITING ALL THAT IS

TO UNFOLD FOR YOU.

AND WHEN YOU WAKE IN THE MORNING, I WILL
LOVE YOU EVEN MORE THAN YESTERDAY.

I'LL WITNESS YOUR BRILLIANT SELF
EMERGE—CREATIVE, UNIQUE, AND ALIVE.

WATCH YOU SLAY YOUR FEARS AS YOU ROUSE
THE RIVERS OF OPPORTUNITY AHEAD OF YOU.

GENTLY WHISPER AND REMIND YOU,

GO WITH THE FLOW, MY LOVE.

I WILL WAIT FOR YOU TO
SHARE WITH ME WHO YOU ARE.

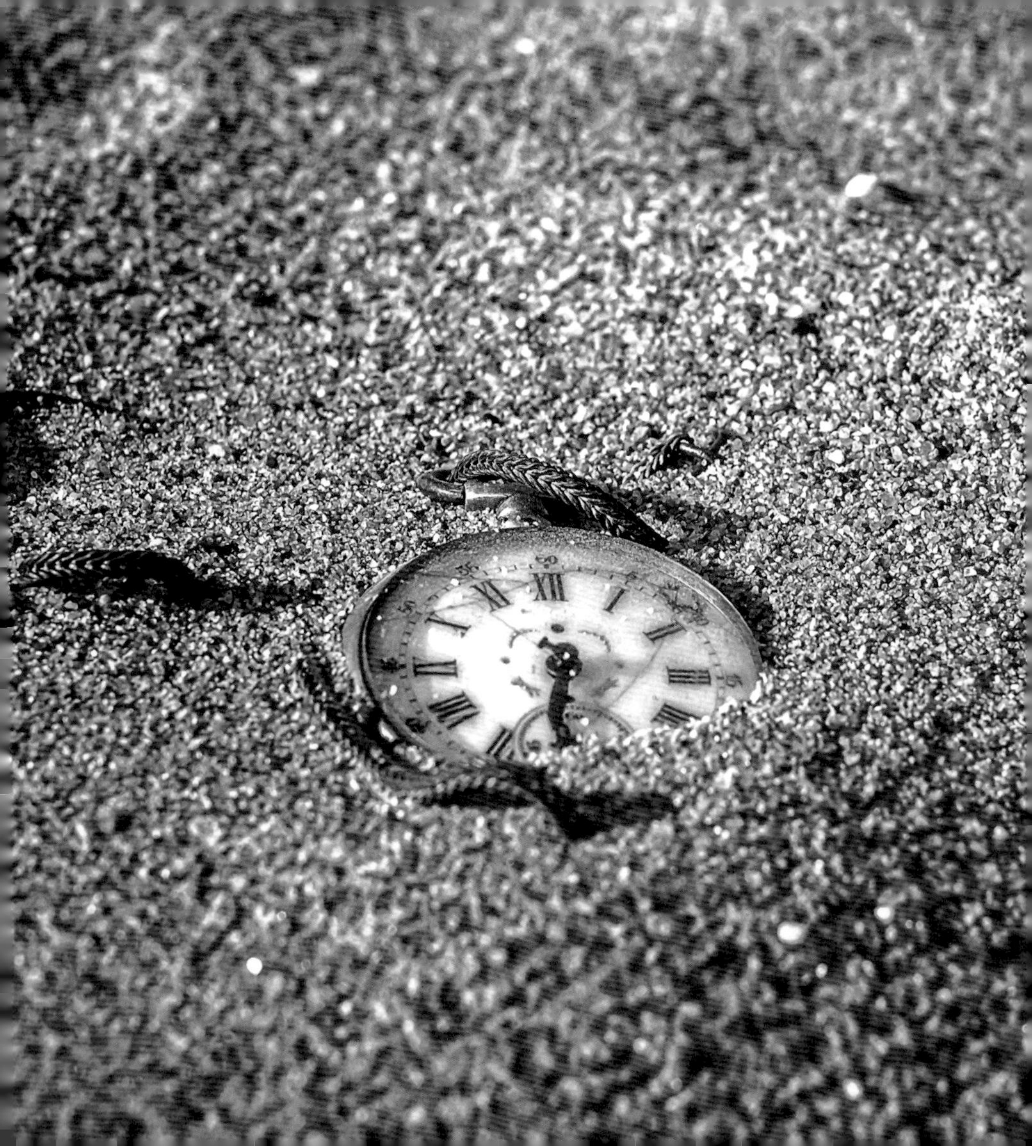

SARAH L. DICKEY

EACH BREATH A GIFT.

EACH SMILE AN EXCHANGE.

EACH SORROW A THREAD OF LIFE
SHARED BETWEEN US.

ODE TO LOVE

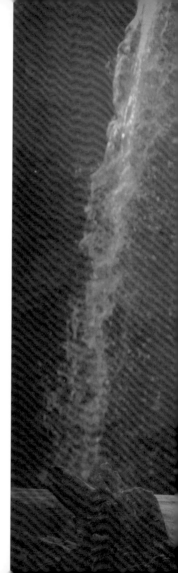

EACH MOMENT A DAZZLING
EXPERIENCE OF YOUR ESSENCE

TUCKED FOREVER IN THE
REMEMBRANCE OF MY HEART.

AND THE DAYS WILL TURN INTO YEARS,
AND MY HEART WILL SIMPLY ADORE YOU
BECAUSE YOU ARE BECOMING ALL THAT
YOU WERE MEANT TO BE.

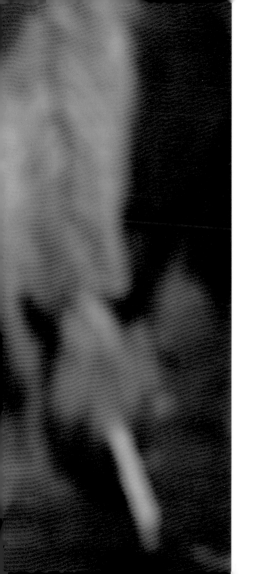

YOU WILL INSPIRE OTHERS.

REMIND THEM WHO THEY TRULY ARE.

UNFOLD INTO THE MYSTERIES OF YOUR LIFE
WITH COMPASSION, JOY, AND GRACE.

WAKE UP DAY AFTER DAY AND
YEAR AFTER YEAR.

YOU WILL TRAVEL TO FAR-OFF LANDS
AND COME BACK CHANGED.

RETURN TO THE WALLS OF YOUR HOME, SEEING LIFE IN DIFFERENT PATTERNS AND TEXTURES.

GO TO COLLEGE, START A BUSINESS,
WRITE A BOOK, SING A SONG, OR BE SO BUSY
LIVING THE LIFE YOU WERE MEANT TO LIVE
THAT YOU'LL BE ALL THE ABOVE
AND SO MUCH MORE.

THERE IS NO BOX AROUND YOUR LIFE,
MY LOVE.

YOU ARE MEANT TO EXPRESS, IMAGINE,
CREATE, AND LIVE THE LIFE OF YOUR DREAMS.

AND I LOVE YOU BECAUSE YOU EXIST
IN THE WORLD, SPEAKING A
LANGUAGE ALL YOUR OWN.

YOU WILL SHARE THIS LANGUAGE WITH MANY.

AND THE FLUENCY OF YOUR LIFE WILL
ENCOURAGE OTHERS TO SPEAK
THEIR NATIVE TONGUE.

YOU WILL WELCOME OTHERS INTO YOUR
ESSENCE AND SCATTER COMPASSION WITH
YOUR ACTIONS.

YOU WILL BE AN INSTRUMENT OF PEACE.

AN AGENT OF CHANGE.

A DREAMER OF DREAMS.

A LOVER OF LIFE.

A SCULPTOR OF PAIN.

AN ALCHEMIST OF FEARS.

A HEART DEVOTED TO THE
PILGRIMAGE OF SERVING THE WORLD.

TRANSLATE, CONSTRUCT, ENVISION, AND
INVEST IN YOUR HEART, MY LOVE.

EXCAVATE OLD BELIEFS.

ENGINEER NEW WAYS OF BEING.

ELEVATE THE WORLD AROUND YOU.

EMPOWER SOULS WITH YOUR WORDS.

SUPERCHARGE YOUR LIFE WITH DEVOTION.

REST IN THE SIMPLICITY OF BEING YOU.

HONOR THE ECSTASY OF YOUR DIVINE SPIRIT.

TRUST THE TIMING.

SAY YES WHEN YOU MEAN IT
AND NO WHEN YOU DON'T.

KNOW THAT I WILL ALWAYS LOVE YOU

AS YOU ARE BEING YOU.

GONE ARE THE DAYS OF LOVING YOU IF ONLY.

GONE ARE THE DAYS OF LOVING YOU BECAUSE.

GONE ARE THE SEASONS OF WANTING YOU TO
BE OTHER THAN YOU ARE.

YOU ALWAYS REMAIN IN MY HEART . . .

NO MATTER THE AGE OR STAGE OF YOUR LIFE.

I WILL LOVE YOU BECAUSE
YOU ARE JUST AS YOU ARE!

AND TO ME THAT IS ALL I COULD
HAVE EVER HOPED FOR.

SARAH DICKEY IS A LOVER OF LIFE. HER ENCHANTMENT WITH WORDS BEGAN AS A YOUNG GIRL, AND SHE HAS CONTINUED TO CULTIVATE THIS DEVOTION INTO ADULTHOOD. SARAH HOLDS A BACHELOR OF ARTS DEGREE FROM YOUNGSTOWN STATE UNIVERSITY AND A MASTER'S DEGREE IN EDUCATION FROM MALONE UNIVERSITY. THROUGHOUT HER LIFE SHE HAS PASSIONATELY PURSUED VARIOUS PATHS OF PERSONAL GROWTH AND PROFESSIONAL DEVELOPMENT. YOU'LL OFTEN FIND SARAH BEHIND THE LENS OF HER CAMERA, TEACHING A YOGA CLASS, BLOGGING ABOUT LIFE, OR DESIGNING NEW POSSIBILITIES TO SHARE HER LIGHT WITH THE WORLD. THE WORDS OF RUMI HAVE ENCOURAGED HER TO FOLLOW HER DREAMS: "WHAT YOU SEEK IS SEEKING YOU." SARAH BELIEVES THAT BY LIVING THIS WAY WE CAN CHANGE THE TRAJECTORY OF OUR LIVES. SHE RESIDES IN THE NORTHEAST. *ODE TO LOVE* IS SARAH'S FIRST BOOK.

PHOTO BY MELISSA G. ILER